I0518263

THE BEAST WITH A BILLION BUREAUCRATS

How the United States Built an Untouchable Administrative State

MATTHEW P. SILBERMAN

Copyright

© 2026 Matthew P. Silberman

All rights reserved.

No part of this book may be reproduced, stored in a retrieval system, or transmitted in any form or by any means electronic, mechanical, photocopying, recording, or otherwise without prior written permission from the publisher, except for brief quotations in critical reviews or scholarly works.

This book is a work of independent analysis and interpretation. Facts are facts and represented as so, everything else is opinion of the author. It is not affiliated with, endorsed by, or representative of any government agency, political party, or institution.

Printed in the United States of America.

Artwork by Matthew Silberman & ChatGpt

www.alchemyandartistry.com

Rev.1

ISBN: 979-8-9947580-0-7

Dedication

**For My Muse, My Friend, My Wife
The Lady Tanya Notkoff**

And

**My Fur Kids
Gigi, Felix, Miriam, Eli and Razcull**

"The accumulation of all powers, legislative, executive, and judiciary, in the same hands... may justly be pronounced the very definition of tyranny."

~ James Madison, Federalist No. 47

"The more numerous the laws, the more the corrupt government."

~Tacitus

Table of Contents - I

Preface

This book is not an argument for or against any political ideology. It is not a defense of one party or an indictment of another. It is an attempt to describe, as clearly and neutrally as possible, how the American government evolved into a structure that no longer behaves the way its designers intended.

The administrative state did not emerge from a single decision, a single law, or a single moment. It emerged from thousands of small choices, each rational in isolation, each understandable in context that accumulated into a system with its own logic, incentives, and survival instincts.

This book is an attempt to map that system.

It is written for readers who sense that elections matter less than they once did, that institutions behave independently of public will, and that the machinery of government has become too complex for any one branch, or any one person to control.

It is not a call to despair.

It is a call to clarity.

Because only when we see the system as it truly is can we begin to understand what it means for the future.

Introduction

The United States was designed to be governed by tension, a balance of powers, a competition of ambitions, a structure in which no single institution could dominate the others. But over the last century, that balance shifted. Power migrated away from elected officials and toward a permanent administrative apparatus that outlasts elections, absorbs political energy, and governs through continuity rather than consent.

This book tells the story of how that happened.

It begins with Congress, which delegated its authority to agencies. It moves through the courts, which deferred to those agencies. It examines the bureaucracy, which became the system's memory and mind. It explores the media, the states, and the financial architecture that reinforced the administrative state's dominance. And it ends with the recognition that the system now operates according to its own logic, not the logic of elections, not the logic of the Constitution, and not the logic of democratic accountability.

This is not a story of villains.

It is a story of incentives.

It is a story of complexity.

It is a story of emergence.

And it is a story that every citizen deserves to understand.

Chapter 1
Congress Abandoned Its Power: The Birth and First Feeding of the Beast

Americans often call the media the "fourth branch of government." That's a cultural metaphor, a commentary on influence, not constitutional structure. The *real* fourth branch, the one the Founders never imagined and never authorized, is the **administrative state**: the vast network of federal agencies that write rules, enforce them, and adjudicate disputes under them.

This chapter explains how Congress, the branch designed to be closest to the people, slowly surrendered its authority and fed the creature that now governs in its place.

The Constitutional Blueprint And the Betrayal

The Founders built Congress to be the engine of lawmaking. Article I is long, detailed, and explicit: Congress writes the laws, controls the purse, and checks the Executive.

But over the 20th century, Congress discovered a political loophole:

If you delegate power, you also delegate blame.

Instead of writing detailed statutes, Congress increasingly passed broad, open-ended laws that handed real decision-making to agencies. This wasn't an accident. It was a strategy.

Delegation as Political Self-Preservation

Delegation solved Congress's biggest problem: accountability.

- Popular outcomes? Congress takes credit.
- Unpopular outcomes? Blame the agency.
- Policy failure? Hold a hearing and act outraged.
- Policy success? Claim it was the intent all along.

Delegation became a **shield**, and the administrative state became the **scapegoat**.
This was the first feeding of the Beast.

The Legislative Seeds of Delegation

Below are the major acts that opened the door to the administrative state. Each one will get its own deep dive later, but here they serve as the structural milestones.

1. The Interstate Commerce Act (1887)

Created the first modern regulatory agency and established the idea that Congress could hand ongoing regulatory authority to an expert body.

2. The Federal Reserve Act (1913)

Delegated monetary authority to an independent board, a massive shift of economic power away from elected officials.

3. The Federal Trade Commission Act (1914)

Created an agency with quasi-legislative and quasi-judicial powers, normalizing the idea that agencies could write rules and enforce them.

4. The New Deal Statutes (1933–1938)

A wave of laws, like the National Industrial Recovery Act, delegated sweeping authority to agencies to manage entire sectors of the economy.

5. The Administrative Procedure Act (1946)

Codified the administrative state. It didn't limit agency power, it legitimized it, giving agencies a formal process for rule making and adjudication.

6. The Clean Air Act (1970) & Clean Water Act (1972)
Gave EPA broad authority to set national standards, often with vague statutory language that left the real policymaking to the agency.

7. The Dodd-Frank Act (2010)
Created new agencies, like the Consumer Financial Protection Bureau, with unprecedented independence from congressional appropriations and presidential control.

Each of these laws expanded the Beast's body, new limbs, new organs, new instincts.

The Rise of the Real Fourth Branch

By mid-century, agencies were exercising all three powers of government:

- **Legislative:** writing binding regulations
- **Executive:** enforcing those regulations
- **Judicial:** adjudicating disputes under those regulations

The Founders would have seen this as a constitutional nightmare, the concentration of power they feared most. Congress saw it as a convenience.

The Incentive Problem

Congress has no incentive to reclaim its power. In fact, it has every incentive **NOT** to.

Reclaiming power means:

- writing detailed laws
- taking responsibility
- facing backlash
- making hard choices
- being accountable

Delegation means:

- avoiding blame
- avoiding expertise
- avoiding responsibility
- avoiding political risk

The Founders assumed ambition would counteract ambition. They never imagined ambition would outsource itself.

The Result: A Government That Governs Itself

Once Congress abdicated, the administrative state filled the vacuum. Agencies became:
- the writers of law
- the interpreters of law
- the enforcers of law

Congress became:

- a spectator
- a commentator
- a fundraising machine
- a performance stage

The Beast didn't seize power. It was handed over willingly.

Why This Matters

When Congress gives away power:

- Elections matter less.
- Accountability evaporates.
- Agencies become permanent.

- Policy becomes insulated from public will.
- The administrative state becomes the true center of gravity.

This is the first step in understanding how the United States built a system that outlives presidents, ignores elections, and protects itself from oversight.

The Beast was born when Congress stopped being a branch of government and became a theater of government. The administrative state didn't rise because bureaucrats were ambitious. It rose because Congress was cowardly. The Founders built a system that required constant maintenance and Congress walked away from the controls washing their hands of their responsibilities.

CHAPTER 2
The Courts Forged the Shield: How Judicial Doctrine Armored the Administrative State

Congress may have fed the Beast, but it was the courts that gave it armor.

The Founders imagined the judiciary as the "least dangerous branch," a body with "neither force nor will, but merely judgment." Yet over the 20th century, the Supreme Court constructed a legal framework that insulated federal agencies from meaningful challenge. Not intentionally. Not maliciously. But systematically.

This chapter traces how judicial doctrine, case by case, decade by decade, transformed agencies from mere administrative helpers into quasi-sovereign entities with the power to interpret, enforce, and effectively create law.

The administrative state didn't seize this power.

The courts handed it to them.

The Founders' Blind Spot

The Constitution never mentions agencies. It never imagines them.

It never anticipates a world where Congress would outsource its authority to unelected experts.

The Founders assumed:

- Congress would write the laws
- The Executive would enforce them
- The Judiciary would interpret them

They did not foresee a fourth entity, a hybrid that would do all three.

So when federal agencies emerged in the late 19th and early 20th centuries, the courts had no constitutional blueprint for how to treat them. They improvised. And improvisation in constitutional law has dire consequences.

The Early Struggle: Agencies as Constitutional Strangers

In the early 1900s, the Supreme Court was skeptical of broad delegation. It struck down parts of the New Deal in cases like *Schechter Poultry* (1935), warning that Congress could not hand "unfettered discretion" to the Executive.
But this resistance was short-lived.

Political pressure, economic crisis, and institutional caution pushed the Court toward a new posture: **deference.**

The Court didn't want to run the country. It didn't want to micromanage agencies. It didn't want to be blamed for economic collapse.

So it stepped back.

And in stepping back, it created a vacuum that federal agencies filled.

The Doctrines That Built the Shield

Below are the core judicial doctrines that insulated the administrative state. Each will get its own in depth later, but here they serve as the spine of the Beast's armor.

1. The "Intelligible Principle" Doctrine *J.W. Hampton* (1928)

The Court ruled that Congress can delegate power, as long as it provides an "intelligible principle."

This standard is so low, it's practically subterranean.

Effect:

Congress can hand agencies enormous discretion with minimal guidance.

2. The Death of the Legislative Veto *INS v. Chadha* (1983)

Congress used to be able to overturn agency actions with a simple one-house vote. *Chadha* struck that down.

Effect:

Congress lost its fastest, simplest tool for reining in agencies.

3. Chevron Deference *Chevron v. NRDC* (1984)

The Court held that if a statute is ambiguous, courts must defer to the agency's interpretation, as long as it's "reasonable."

Effect:

Agencies effectively gained the power to interpret and therefore shape the law.

For forty years, Chevron was the administrative state's Excalibur.

4. Auer Deference *Auer v. Robbins* (1997)

Courts must defer to an agency's interpretation of its *own* regulations.

Effect:

Agencies write the rules and then get to decide what those rules mean.

This is the judicial equivalent of letting a referee write the rulebook and then interpret penalties during the game.

5. Hard Look Review *State Farm* **(1983)**

Courts review agency decisions only for extreme irrationality.

Effect:

As long as an agency produces a thick administrative record, courts rarely intervene.

Paperwork became armor, the red tape that clogs the gears of everything.

The Courts' Motivations: Why They Stepped Back

The Judiciary didn't empower agencies out of ideological zeal. It did so because:

- Judges lacked technical expertise.
- Agencies had armies of specialists.
- Courts feared being blamed for policy failures.
- Deference seemed like the "neutral" position.
- The administrative state grew too large to supervise case-by-case.

The courts didn't want to govern. So they let the agencies govern.

This was not judicial humility.

It was judicial abdication.

The Consequence: Agencies Became the Interpreters of Their Own Power

Once the courts embraced deference, agencies gained:

- the power to define statutory ambiguity
- the power to interpret their own rules
- the power to justify their own decisions
- the power to expand their own jurisdiction

The Judiciary became a spectator. The administrative state became the author of its own authority.

This is how the Beast grew teeth.

The Illusion of Oversight

The courts still hear challenges to agency actions. They still issue opinions. They still appear to be referees.

But the reality is different.

When the standard is "defer unless unreasonable," the referee is really just watching the game.

When the agency writes the rules, the referee is reading from the agency's script.

When the agency interprets its own rules, the referee is bound by the agency's dictionary. The courts didn't just fail to restrain the administrative state.

They legitimized it.

The Turning Point: Chevron's Fall

In 2024, the Supreme Court overturned Chevron in *Loper Bright v. Raimondo*.

This was a seismic shift but it came after four decades of agency expansion.

Removing Chevron is like removing the scaffolding after the skyscraper is already built.

The structure remains.

The Beast remains.

Congress created the Beast, gave it food.

The courts armored it.

Through deference doctrines, permissive delegation standards, and the dismantling of congressional oversight tools, the Judiciary transformed agencies into a legally insulated fourth branch of government, one the Founders never imagined and the Constitution never authorized.

CHAPTER 3
The Rise of the Permanent Bureaucracy: How Career Officials Became the Beast's Nervous System

Congress fed the Beast.

The courts armored it.

But neither explains how the Beast learned to *think*.

That came from the rise of the **permanent bureaucracy,** the <u>unelected</u>, largely unremovable class of career officials who outlast presidents, outmaneuver political appointees, and maintain institutional continuity across decades. They are not villains. They are not heroes. They are the nervous system of the administrative state, and they are the reason the system behaves like a living organism rather than a collection of offices.

This chapter traces how the federal workforce evolved from a small clerical corps into a sprawling, self-protecting, self-perpetuating administrative class that no election can meaningfully dislodge.

The Founders Never Imagined a Permanent Bureaucracy

The Founders assumed government would be:

- small
- temporary
- staffed by citizens who rotated in and out
- supervised by elected officials

They did not imagine:

- millions of federal employees
- qualified immunity
- lifetime tenure
- unions
- civil service protections
- specialized technical corps
- agencies with their own internal cultures

The Constitution is silent on bureaucracy because the Founders assumed it would remain small enough to be supervised by Congress and the President. They were wrong.

The Spoils System: The First Attempt at Control

In the 19th century, federal jobs were political rewards.
Presidents appointed loyalists; new administrations
cleaned house. This system was corrupt, chaotic, and
often incompetent but it had one virtue:
The bureaucracy was not permanent.
Every election reshaped the administrative workforce.
Every president could impose direction.
Every official knew their job depended on political
accountability.
But the assassination of President James Garfield in
1881, by a disgruntled office seeker, triggered a national
backlash against patronage.
Reform was coming.

The Pendleton Act (1883): The Birth of the Modern Bureaucracy

The Pendleton Civil Service Reform Act created:

- merit-based hiring
- competitive exams
- protections against political firing

It was meant to professionalize government.

It succeeded but it also created the first layer of permanence.

Over time, Congress expanded civil service protections until the majority of federal employees were shielded from political removal.

The intention was noble.

The consequence was structural.

A new class emerged: **career officials who outlast every administration.**

The New Deal: Bureaucracy Becomes a Profession

The Great Depression and World War II transformed the federal workforce from a clerical service into a professionalized administrative class.

Agencies needed:

- economists
- engineers
- scientists
- lawyers
- analysts
- inspectors

- regulators

These were not temporary roles.
They required expertise, continuity, and institutional memory.
By the 1950s, the federal bureaucracy was no longer a job.
It was a career.
By the 1970s, it was a profession.
By the 1990s, it was a culture.

Civil Service Protections Harden Into Armor

Over the 20th century, civil service protections expanded into a near-impenetrable shield:

- strict rules for firing
- lengthy appeals processes
- union representation
- whistleblower complexities
- procedural hurdles
- political retaliation prohibitions

These protections were designed to prevent abuse.
They also made it extremely difficult to remove underperforming or resistant officials.
The result was a workforce that is:

- stable
- insulated
- self-protecting
- resistant to rapid change

This is not conspiracy.
It is institutional design.

The Bureaucratic Mind: Culture as Power

Every large organization develops a culture.
The federal bureaucracy is no different.

Its culture values:

- continuity over disruption
- procedure over improvisation
- caution over risk
- precedent over innovation
- internal loyalty over external pressure

This culture is not ideological and it is not rare.
It is structural.

It rewards those who:

- protect the agency

- maintain stability
- avoid scandal
- preserve jurisdiction
- defend budgets

It punishes those who:

- challenge norms
- threaten internal alliances
- expose inefficiencies
- disrupt established processes

This is how the Beast learned to think.

The Bureaucracy Outlives Elections

Political appointees are temporary:

- Cabinet secretaries last two to four years
- deputy secretaries last one to three years
- agency heads often last less than eighteen months

Career officials last twenty to fifty years.
This creates a simple dynamic.
Appointees come to lead agencies they do not understand.
Career officials lead agencies they do not control.

The bureaucracy does not defy presidents.
It outlasts them.

The Bureaucratic Veto

Career officials have subtle tools to resist political direction:

- slow-walking
- reinterpretation
- procedural delay
- "lost" paperwork
- endless review cycles
- risk-averse legal opinions
- selective enforcement
- strategic leaks
- lame duck congress

These are not acts of rebellion.
They are acts of institutional self-preservation.
The Beast protects itself.

The Iron Triangle: Bureaucrats, Lobbyists, and Congress

The permanent bureaucracy does not operate alone.
It forms alliances:

- **Agencies** want stable budgets and expanded authority.
- **Lobbyists** want favorable regulations.
- **Congress** wants campaign donations and political cover.

This triangle creates a feedback loop:

- Agencies write rules.
- Lobbyists influence them.
- Congress funds them.
- Agencies enforce them.

THE PUBLIC IS NOT PART OF THIS LOOP.

The Result: A Self-Perpetuating Administrative Class

By the late 20th century, the federal bureaucracy had become:

- too large to supervise
- too specialized to replace
- too protected to reform
- too interconnected to dismantle
- too essential to ignore

It is not a conspiracy.
It is an ecosystem.

A permanent administrative class that:

- outlives elections
- shapes policy
- protects itself
- resists disruption
- maintains continuity
- expands its own authority

This is the nervous system of the Beast.

The administrative state is not powerful because bureaucrats are malicious.

It is powerful because bureaucrats are permanent.

Congress created the Beast, gave it food.
The courts armored it.
The bureaucracy gave it a mind.

CHAPTER 4
The Information Monopoly: How Agencies Became the Gatekeepers of Reality

Power doesn't just come from laws, budgets, or personnel.

Power comes from **information**.

Who gathers it.

Who interprets it.

Who controls access to it.

Who decides what counts as "expertise."

In the modern administrative state, federal agencies became the arbiters of knowledge itself. They control the data elected officials rely on, the technical analyses courts defer to, and the regulatory models industries must obey. This monopoly on information didn't emerge overnight. It grew slowly, layer by layer, until the administrative state became the only institution capable of explaining the world it regulates.

This chapter explores how agencies became the gatekeepers of reality and why no branch of government can meaningfully challenge them without first breaking their informational dominance.

The Founders' World Was Simple, Ours Is Not

In 1787, the federal government didn't need:

- climate models
- epidemiological forecasts
- financial stress tests
- nuclear safety analyses
- environmental impact statements
- cybersecurity threat assessments

The Founders lived in a world where information was:

- local
- observable
- simple
- slow

Modern governance is none of those things.
As the world grew more complex, Congress and the courts increasingly relied on agencies to provide the expertise they lacked. This reliance became dependence. Dependence became deference. Deference became dominance.

The Rise of the Expert Class

The administrative state's information monopoly began with the rise of the **expert class** economists, scientists, engineers, analysts, and lawyers, who staffed the agencies created during the Progressive Era and the New Deal.
These experts:

- collected data
- built models
- wrote technical reports
- interpreted scientific findings
- advised policymakers

Over time, agencies became the only institutions with the capacity to understand the systems they regulated.
Congress didn't have the staff.
The courts didn't have the training.
The public didn't have the access.
Expertise became another form of power.

The Information Loop: Agencies as Both Source and Interpreter

Agencies don't just gather information.
They **define** it.

They decide:

- what data to collect
- how to measure it
- which models to use
- which assumptions to embed
- which uncertainties to disclose
- which risks to emphasize

This creates a closed loop:

- Agencies gather the data.
- Agencies interpret the data they collected.
- Agencies justify their rules using the data they interpreted.
- Courts defer to the agencies' interpretation of the data.
- Congress relies on the agencies' reports to write new laws.

The agency becomes both the scientist and the peer reviewer, the analyst and the auditor, the witness and the judge.
This is not oversight.
It is epistemic capture.

The Administrative Record: Paperwork as Armor

Under the Administrative Procedure Act (APA), agencies must justify their decisions with an "administrative record." Over time, this record became a shield, a mountain of technical documents that courts are reluctant to second-guess.

A typical major rule might include:

- thousands of pages of analysis
- economic impact models
- environmental assessments
- risk projections
- cost-benefit calculations
- scientific literature reviews

To challenge a rule, a plaintiff must show the agency acted "arbitrarily or capriciously." But when the agency controls the data, the models, and the narrative, this standard becomes nearly impossible to meet.
Paperwork becomes armor.
Complexity becomes insulation.
Expertise becomes authority.

Congress Becomes Dependent

Congress once had its own sources of expertise:

- the Office of Technology Assessment (defunded in 1995)
- robust committee staff
- independent research arms

But over the last forty years, Congress hollowed out its own capacity. Staff levels dropped. Expertise eroded. Committees became political stages rather than analytical bodies.

Today, Congress relies on agencies for:

- technical briefings
- data analysis
- regulatory impact assessments
- scientific interpretation
- economic modeling

This dependence means Congress cannot meaningfully oversee the administrative state. It doesn't have the tools.

The Beast writes the reports.
Congress reads them and sometimes even understands them.

The Courts Become Dependent

Judges are generalists.
Agencies are specialists.
Courts faced with:

- complex environmental models
- financial risk algorithms
- epidemiological projections
- cybersecurity threat matrices
- energy grid simulations

...defer.
Not because they want to.
Because they have to.
The judiciary cannot independently verify the technical claims agencies make. So it relies on the administrative record, the very record the agency created to justify its own decisions.
This is how deference becomes inevitability.

The Public Is Locked Out

The public cannot meaningfully challenge agency expertise because:

- The data is often inaccessible.
- The models are proprietary.
- The assumptions are buried.
- The analyses require advanced training.
- The process is opaque.
- The timelines are short.
- The cost of litigation is enormous.

This creates a democratic paradox:

- the people are governed by rules they cannot understand
- justified by data they cannot access
- interpreted by experts they cannot question

The Beast speaks a language only it can understand.

The Information Monopoly Becomes Self-Reinforcing

Once agencies control information, they control:

- the narrative
- the justification
- the oversight
- the litigation
- the policymaking

This monopoly is self-reinforcing:

- Agencies justify their own expansion with their own data.
- Courts defer because agencies are the experts.
- Congress legislates based on agency reports.
- The public accepts agency claims because no alternative exists.

The administrative state becomes the only institution capable of explaining the world it regulates.
This is how the Beast became the gatekeeper of reality.
The administrative state's power does not come from force.
It comes from knowledge or rather, from controlling the production and interpretation of knowledge.
Congress created the Beast, gave it food.
The courts armored it.
The bureaucracy gave it a mind.
And the information monopoly gave it a voice.

CHAPTER 5
The Inter-Agency Shield: How Federal Institutions Learned to Protect the Beast

By now, the Beast has taken shape. But even with all that, the administrative state would still be vulnerable if its parts operated independently. It would be a giant, yes, but a giant with exposed joints, soft organs, and no coordination.

That is not the creature we face.

Over the 20th century, federal agencies developed a powerful instinct: **mutual protection**. They learned to defend one another, share information strategically, coordinate narratives, and close ranks when threatened. This wasn't a conspiracy. It was an evolution, the natural behavior of institutions that depend on stability, continuity, and mutual survival.

This chapter explores how the administrative state became a federated organism, each part reinforcing the others, forming a shield that no single branch of government can easily penetrate.

The Logic of Institutional Self-Defense

Every institution develops mechanisms to protect itself. But the administrative state is unique because:

- Its components are legally insulated.
- Its workforce is permanent.
- Its authority is diffuse.
- Its incentives align internally.
- Its oversight is fragmented.

This creates a simple evolutionary rule: If one agency is threatened, all agencies are threatened.
And so they defend each other.

DOJ: The Beast's Legal Shield

The Department of Justice is often described as the nation's top law enforcement body. In reality, it functions as the **legal immune system** of the administrative state, the institution that protects federal agencies from external scrutiny, internal accountability, and meaningful legal consequences.
This is not ideological.
It is structural.
Below is how DOJ maintains that power.

1. DOJ Controls All Litigation Against the Federal Government

When a federal agency is sued, it does not hire its own lawyers. It does not face independent scrutiny. It does not answer directly to the courts.

DOJ steps in and takes over.

This means:

- Agencies never face independent legal representation.
- DOJ decides the strategy, tone, and scope of the defense.
- DOJ can delay, narrow, or bury cases.
- DOJ can settle without admitting wrongdoing.
- DOJ can appeal indefinitely, exhausting challengers.

The Beast never fights with one limb.
It fights with its entire body.

2. DOJ Selectively Enforces and Selectively Refuses to Enforce

One of DOJ's most powerful tools is its discretion. The Department decides:

- which crimes to prosecute
- which agencies to investigate

- which officials to indict
- which scandals to pursue
- which cases to ignore

And the pattern is unmistakable.
DOJ rarely prosecutes federal officials for crimes committed while working in their official capacity. Because doing so would:

- set precedent
- expose internal processes
- weaken agency authority
- invite further scrutiny
- threaten the administrative state's legitimacy

The system protects its own.

3. DOJ Uses "Institutional Interests" to Override Justice

Inside DOJ, there is a phrase that appears in internal memos and legal briefs:

"The institutional interests of the United States."

This does not mean the public.
It does not mean the Constitution.
It does not mean justice.

It means:

- preserving agency authority
- defending Executive power
- avoiding precedent that limits federal discretion
- preventing disclosure of internal processes
- maintaining the administrative state's autonomy

When DOJ invokes "institutional interests," it means, the Beast must be protected.

4. DOJ Controls Access to Evidence and Withholds It Strategically

When Congress demands documents, DOJ decides:

- what to release
- what to redact
- what to delay
- what to deny

When courts request records, DOJ argues:

- ongoing investigation
- national security
- deliberative process
- executive authority
- privilege

These claims often have little to do with actual security.
They are tools of **institutional opacity**.
The Beast survives by controlling information.
DOJ is the gatekeeper.

5. DOJ Uses Delay as a Weapon

Time is one of DOJ's most effective tools.

The Department can:

- drag out investigations
- slow walk document production
- file endless procedural motions
- appeal every adverse ruling
- wait out political cycles
- *exhaust plaintiffs financially*

For citizens, watchdog groups, or whistleblowers, delay is defeat. For the administrative state, delay is victory.
The Beast does not need to win in a sprint
It turns most cases into ultra marathons.

6. DOJ Protects Agencies Through "No-Fault Settlements"

When wrongdoing is undeniable, DOJ often negotiates settlements that:

- impose no personal liability
- admit no fault
- require no structural reform
- seal key documents
- require non disclosure agreements
- avoid precedent
- preserve agency authority

These settlements create the appearance of accountability without the substance.
The Beast sheds a little skin like reactive armor.
The threat is deflected away or destroyed, causing little damage, and is easily replaced.

7. DOJ Defers Prosecution of Federal Actors Indefinitely

When federal officials commit crimes that would land private citizens in prison, DOJ often uses:

- deferred prosecution agreements
- internal discipline
- administrative remedies
- quiet reassignments
- early retirements

These are not punishments.
They are pressure valves.
They protect the system from scandal while avoiding the dangerous precedent of holding federal actors criminally liable.
The Beast punishes disobedience.
It does not punish itself.

8. DOJ Shapes the Narrative Through Public Statements

When scandals break, DOJ controls the narrative:

- "We cannot comment on ongoing investigations."

- "We found no evidence of criminal intent."
- "The matter has been referred for internal review."
- "We take these allegations seriously."

These statements are not explanations. They are shields. They buy time. They calm the public. They protect the agencies.

They prevent any momentum for reform.

The Beast speaks through the DOJ and it speaks in riddles.

9. DOJ's Loyalty Is Structural, Not Political

DOJ does not protect agencies because of ideology.
It protects them because:

- Precedent is dangerous.
- Accountability is destabilizing.
- Agencies are part of the Executive Branch.
- Weakening one weakens all.
- Transparency is risky.
- The administrative state depends on internal solidarity.

DOJ's loyalty is not to presidents.

Not to Congress.

Not to the public.

Its loyalty is to the continuity of federal power itself.

The Beast protects its heart.

OMB and OIRA: The Coordinators of the Shield

The Office of Management and Budget (OMB) and its regulatory review arm, (OIRA), act as internal referees. Their role is not to restrain agencies, it is to coordinate them.

Through:

- harmonizing regulatory agendas
- mediating inter-agency disputes
- protecting budgets
- ensuring consistent messaging
- preventing contradictory rules

Externally, agencies may appear fragmented.

Internally, they speak with one voice.

Inspectors General: The Illusion of Internal Policing

Inspectors General (IGs) are portrayed as watchdogs. In reality, they are:

- underfunded
- understaffed
- politically constrained
- dependent on agency cooperation
- limited in jurisdiction
- vulnerable to retaliation

IGs expose misconduct, but they cannot enforce consequences.

Their reports often become:

- political theater
- bureaucratic paperwork
- recommendations without teeth

The Beast tolerates IGs because they provide the theater of oversight with zero substance.

Inter-Agency Alliances: The Quiet Networks of Mutual Survival

Agencies form alliances based on:

- shared missions
- overlapping jurisdictions
- common enemies
- budgetary interests
- political pressures

These alliances create a web of mutual reinforcement.
If one agency's authority is challenged, others step in to defend the underlying principle.
The Beast protects its heads.

The Budgetary Immune System

Congress controls the purse strings in theory.
In practice, agencies protect their budgets through:

- coordinated lobbying
- alliances with special interest groups
- strategic leaks
- public-facing narratives
- pressure on congressional committees

Budget cuts are treated as existential threats.
The Beast defends its food source.

The Revolving Door: The Human Shield

The revolving door between:

- agencies
- lobbyists
- think tanks
- regulated industries
- congressional staff
- consulting firms

...creates a shared professional culture.

People move between these institutions, carrying:

- relationships
- loyalties
- institutional memory
- policy preferences

This creates a human network that reinforces the administrative state's worldview. It is not corruption. It is alignment.

The Beast reproduces through human careers.

Crisis as Opportunity

Crises strengthen the inter-agency shield.
During:

- wars
- recessions
- pandemics
- natural disasters
- security threats

...agencies gain:

- emergency powers
- expanded budgets
- extended public deference
- thicker political insulation

After the crisis ends, the powers remain.
The Beast grows during storms.

The Punishment of Dissent

Agencies do not tolerate internal threats.
Whistleblowers face:

- career stagnation
- reassignment
- legal pressure
- social isolation
- bureaucratic retaliation

External critics face:

- selective enforcement
- regulatory scrutiny
- narrative framing
- procedural obstacles

This is not ideological.
It is structural.
The Beast protects itself from infection.

The Result: A Federated Organism

By the 21st century, the administrative state has become
a networked organism:

- DOJ defends it.
- OMB coordinates it.
- IGs legitimize it.
- Agencies reinforce each other.
- Congress depends on it.
- Courts defer to it.
- The public cannot penetrate it.

No single agency is sovereign.
The system itself is sovereign.
This is the inter-agency shield, the immune system of the Beast.
The administrative state is not powerful because any one agency is powerful. It is powerful because the agencies protect each other.

Congress created the Beast, gave it food.
The courts armored it.
The bureaucracy gave it a mind.
The information monopoly gave it a voice.
And DOJ gave it an immune system.

CHAPTER 6
The Hollowing of Congress: How the People's Branch Lost the Capacity to Govern

Congress was supposed to be the center of American self-government, the branch closest to the people, the one with the power of the purse, the authority to write laws, and the responsibility to oversee the Executive. The Founders gave Congress more constitutional text, more enumerated powers, and more structural tools than any other branch.

And yet today, Congress is the weakest of the three.

It is not feared.

It is not respected.

It is not effective.

It is a stage, a place for speeches, fundraising, and televised outrage while the real machinery of governance hums along hidden from public view.

This chapter explains how Congress lost the capacity to govern, how it surrendered its oversight powers, and how its decline allowed the administrative state to grow unchecked.

The Founders' Vision: Congress as the Engine of the Republic

The Founders believed Congress would be:

- the primary maker of policy
- jealous of its power
- ambitious
- vigilant against Executive encroachment
- protective of its prerogatives

They assumed members of Congress would fight to preserve their authority.

Instead, Congress learned to survive by giving it away.

The Decline of Congressional Expertise

In the mid-20th century, Congress had:

- robust committee staffs
- subject-matter experts
- independent research arms
- the Office of Technology Assessment (OTA)
- strong legislative support agencies

These institutions allowed Congress to:

51

- write detailed laws
- challenge agency claims
- conduct meaningful oversight
- understand complex policy domains

But beginning in the 1980s and accelerating in the 1990s, Congress **defunded itself** while continuing to give itself pay raises.
Staff levels dropped. Expertise evaporated.
Committees became political stages rather than analytical bodies.

Today, Congress relies on:

- agency briefings
- agency data
- agency models
- agency interpretations

The Beast generates the reports.
Congress reads them, sometimes.

The Collapse of Oversight

Oversight is supposed to be Congress's most powerful tool. But effective oversight requires:

- staff
- expertise
- persistence
- institutional memory
- bipartisan cooperation
- willingness to confront the Executive

Congress has none of these.

Instead, oversight has become:

- performative
- partisan
- episodic
- shallow
- reactive
- media-driven

Hearings are designed for soundbites, not accountability.
Investigations are designed for fundraising, not reform.
The administrative state knows this.
It has learned to wait out the noise.

The Committee System Becomes Theater

Committees were once the engines of legislative craftsmanship.

Today, they are:

- platforms for speeches
- audition stages for cable news
- fundraising tools
- partisan battlegrounds

Members spend more time:

- preparing talking points
- coordinating media hits
- crafting viral moments

…than reading legislation or interrogating agency behavior.
The Beast does not fear theatrics.
It fears competence.
Congress abandoned competence last century.

The Power of the Purse Surrendered

The Constitution gives Congress exclusive control over federal spending.

But over time, Congress:

- outsourced budgeting to the Executive
- relied on continuing resolutions
- abandoned regular appropriations
- allowed agencies to self-fund through fees and fines
- tolerated emergency spending as routine

This means:

- Agencies can operate without annual scrutiny.
- Budgets grow without debate.
- Congress loses leverage.
- Spending becomes automatic.

The Beast feeds itself.

The Rise of Omnibus Bills and the Death of Deliberation

Modern Congress passes:

- thousand-page omnibus bills
- unreadable continuing resolutions
- last-minute spending packages

Members vote on legislation they have not read, written by lobbyists they have no control over, influenced by agencies they do not understand.

This is not lawmaking.

It is legislative outsourcing.

The Beast writes the detailed narratives.

Congress votes along party lines.

The Party Machines Replace Institutional Loyalty

The Founders assumed members of Congress would be loyal to their chamber, defending its authority against the Executive. Instead, members are loyal to:

- their donors
- their media ecosystems
- their reelection campaigns
- their party

This means:

- Congress will not check a president of its own party.

- Congress will not challenge agencies aligned with its agenda.
- Congress will not defend its institutional prerogatives.

The Beast thrives when its supposed overseers are focused on public image and campaign funding.

The Revolving Door Weakens Congressional Independence

Members of Congress and their staff often leave for:

- lobbying firms
- consulting shops
- think tanks
- regulated industries (defense, energy, finance)
- agency positions

This creates:

- incentives to avoid antagonizing agencies
- incentives to maintain relationships
- incentives to preserve the administrative state

Congressional staffers do not want to burn bridges.
They want to build express lanes across them.
The Beast rewards loyalty.

The Decline of Legislative Ambition

The Founders expected Congress to be ambitious.
Modern Congress is risk-averse.

Members avoid:

- writing major legislation
- taking controversial positions
- challenging agency authority
- confronting the Executive
- engaging in long term policy work

Instead, they focus on:

- fundraising
- partisan investigations
- symbolic votes
- social media engagement
- messaging

Ambition has been replaced by interpretive dance performance.
The Beast loves its performers.

The Result: A Legislature in Name Only

By the first quarter of the 21st century, Congress has become:

- too weak to write detailed laws
- too understaffed to understand agency behavior
- too partisan to conduct oversight
- too dependent on agencies for information
- too distracted to defend its own authority

It is a legislature in name, not function.
The administrative state governs. Congress comments.
The Beast does not fear Congress. It barely notices it.
Congress was supposed to be the people's branch, the engine of republican self-government. Instead, it hollowed itself out, surrendered its powers, and became a spectator to the administrative state it created.

Congress created the Beast, gave it food.
The courts armored it.
The bureaucracy gave it a mind.
The information monopoly gave it a voice.

The inter-agency shield gave it immunity.
And Congress's cowardice removed the last meaningful check on its growth.

CHAPTER 7
The Media Mirage: How the Watchdog Lost Its Teeth and Became Part of the Beast's Ecosystem

For more than half a century, some Americans have referred to the media as the "fourth branch of government." Not because it holds constitutional authority, but because it was once the primary watchdog, the institution meant to expose corruption, challenge power, and inform the public.

But the media of today is not the media the Founders imagined. It is not independent. It is not adversarial. It is not structurally incentivized to challenge the administrative state.

Instead, it has become part of the Beast's ecosystem amplifying narratives, shaping public perception, and reinforcing the legitimacy of the very institutions it was meant to scrutinize.

This transformation did not happen by accident. It was engineered through a series of legislative and regulatory changes that reshaped the media landscape, concentrated ownership, and removed the guardrails that once ensured diversity of viewpoint and independence of coverage.

This chapter traces how the watchdog became a mirror reflecting the administrative state's preferred image back to the public.

The Founders' Expectation: A Free Press as a Check on Power

The Founders believed a free press would:

- expose government wrongdoing
- challenge official narratives
- inform the public
- prevent the rise of centralized authority

They assumed the press would be decentralized, competitive, and adversarial.

They did not imagine:

- national media conglomerates
- 24-hour news cycles
- algorithmic amplification
- corporate consolidation
- regulatory capture

The media was supposed to be a counterweight.
Instead, it became a pillar.

The Fairness Doctrine (1949–1987): The First Guardrail

The Fairness Doctrine, created by the FCC in 1949, required broadcasters to:

- cover controversial issues of public importance
- present contrasting viewpoints
- maintain balance in political coverage

It did not mandate neutrality, it mandated diversity of perspective.
For nearly forty years, this doctrine ensured that no single narrative could dominate the airwaves.
But in 1987, the FCC abolished it.
This was the first major turning point.

The Repeal of the Fairness Doctrine (1987): The Opening of the Floodgates

When the Fairness Doctrine was repealed:

- Broadcasters no longer had to present opposing views.
- Partisan programming exploded.
- Nationalized narratives replaced local reporting.
- Ideological silos formed.
- Sensationalism became profitable.

This deregulation did not create propaganda.
It created the conditions for it.
Without the Fairness Doctrine, the media became:

- more polarized
- more nationalized
- more dependent on emotional engagement
- more aligned with political and institutional power

The watchdog lost its muzzle and its responsibility.

The Telecommunications Act of 1996: The Great Consolidation

The Telecommunications Act of 1996 was the most sweeping media deregulation in modern history as it:

- removed limits on how many radio stations one company could own

- relaxed restrictions on television ownership
- allowed cross-ownership of newspapers and broadcast stations
- accelerated mergers and acquisitions
- reduced local control over media markets

The result was immediate and dramatic:

- Local news collapsed.
- Independent stations were absorbed.
- National conglomerates dominated the landscape.
- Editorial diversity shrank.
- Corporate interests shaped coverage.

By the early 2000s, a handful of corporations controlled the majority of American media. This consolidation made the media easier to influence and easier to align with institutional power.

The Rise of Cable News and the 24-Hour Cycle

The 24-hour news cycle changed journalism from:

- investigative reporting
- long-form analysis

- local accountability

…into:

- sensationalism
- narrative reinforcement
- crisis-driven coverage
- constant commentary

Speed replaced accuracy.
Emotion replaced context.
Engagement replaced truth.
The administrative state learned to use this to its advantage.

Agencies discovered that:

- releasing information at strategic times
- framing narratives through press briefings
- leaking selectively
- providing "exclusive access"

…could shape public perception more effectively than any formal communication.
The Beast learned to propagate through the news cycle.

The Digital Revolution and Algorithmic Amplification

The rise of digital media and social platforms created:

- algorithmic bias
- viral misinformation
- rapid narrative shifts
- dependence on engagement metrics
- echo chambers

Traditional media adapted by:

- chasing clicks
- prioritizing outrage
- amplifying official narratives that generated traffic
- relying on agency press releases as ready-made content

This creates the "The Wrap-Up Smear":

1. Agencies release information.
2. Media amplifies it for engagement.
3. Social platforms algorithmically boost it.
4. Public perception shifts.
5. Agencies cite public perception as justification.

The Beast learned to manipulate the algorithm.

The Decline of Investigative Journalism

Investigative journalism is expensive, slow, and adversarial.

Modern media is:

- corporate owned
- consolidated
- profit-driven
- risk-averse

As a result:

- investigative units were downsized
- local reporting collapsed
- national outlets focused on commentary
- agencies faced less scrutiny
- whistleblowers lost platforms

The administrative state became harder to investigate and easier to trust by default.

The Rise of Official Narratives

Agencies learned that controlling the narrative is easier than controlling the facts.

They use:

- press briefings
- controlled leaks
- selective data releases
- embargoed reports
- expert panels
- "anonymous officials"
- crisis framing

Media outlets, dependent on access and speed, often repeat these narratives uncritically. This is not propaganda in the classic sense. It is structural alignment.
The Beast speaks.
The media echoes.

The Legislative and Regulatory Milestones That Enabled Media Capture

Here is the consolidated list of the major legislative and regulatory changes that reshaped the media landscape and weakened its watchdog role:

1. The Fairness Doctrine (1949)
Established viewpoint diversity requirements.

2. Repeal of the Fairness Doctrine (1987)
Removed those requirements, enabling partisan dominance.

3. FCC Ownership Rule Changes (1990s–2000s)
Incrementally relaxed cross-ownership and market concentration limits.

4. The Telecommunications Act of 1996
Allowed massive consolidation of media ownership.

5. Section 230 of the Communications Decency Act (1996)
Enabled social platforms to become dominant distributors of news without liability for content, reshaping the information ecosystem.

6. Digital Millennium Copyright Act (1998)
Accelerated the shift to digital platforms, undermining traditional journalism revenue models.

7. Net Neutrality Repeal (2017)
Increased the influence of large Internet Service Providers over content distribution, further centralizing control.

Each of these changes weakened the media's accountability and strengthened its alignment with institutional power.

The Result: A Watchdog That Became a Black Mirror

In the 21st century, the media has become:

- consolidated
- nationalized
- dependent on official narratives
- driven by engagement
- structurally aligned with federal institutions

It no longer challenges the Beast.
It reflects it in the best light.
The administrative state governs. The media explains why it must.
The media was once the watchdog of democracy. Today, it is part of the administrative ecosystem, a narrative amplifier rather than a check on power.
Congress created the Beast, gave it food.
The courts armored it.
The bureaucracy gave it a mind.
The information monopoly gave it a voice.

The inter-agency shield gave it an immune system. And the media gave it legitimacy.

CHAPTER 8
The States Surrender: How Federal Money Became the Beast's Bloodstream.

The Day a Nation Gave Up Its Currency

If you want to understand how the states became dependents, how federal agencies gained leverage, and how the administrative state grew into a creature too large to restrain, you must begin with the moment the United States surrendered direct control of its currency. That moment came in 1913, with the passage of the Federal Reserve Act.

The Federal Reserve was not created by accident. It was designed by:

- Senator Nelson Aldrich, chair of the National Monetary Commission
- Paul Warburg, whose theories shaped the Fed's architecture
- President Woodrow Wilson, who signed the Act
- A small group of financial and political elites who met secretly at Jekyll Island in 1910 to draft the blueprint

The Federal Reserve was built to stabilize the financial system but its structure was unprecedented:

- It was *independent* of direct political control.
- It could expand or contract the money supply.
- It influenced interest rates, credit, and liquidity.
- It operated through a hybrid public-private network.
- Its decisions were insulated from elections.

For the first time in American history, the nation's currency, the foundation of all economic activity, was placed under the control of an institution *not directly accountable to voters*.
This was the first great surrender of state power.

Because when a government gives up control of its currency, it gives up control of:

- its fiscal destiny
- its economic sovereignty
- its ability to resist federal pressure
- its independence from centralized authority

And when the states gave up control of their currency, they gave up the ability to resist federal funding strings.

This is the beginning of how the states became dependents and how the administrative state gained the financial bloodstream it needed to grow.

The Federal Reserve and the Rise of Fiscal Centralization

The Federal Reserve did not directly control the states. But it reshaped the national economy in ways that made **federal money** the only stable source of funding for state governments.

The Fed's control over:

- interest rates
- liquidity
- credit markets
- inflation
- recession cycles

…meant that state budgets became increasingly vulnerable to national economic conditions they could not influence.

States could no longer:

- stabilize their own economies
- manage their own currency
- control their own credit markets
- buffer themselves from national downturns

This vulnerability created a dependency.
And the federal government filled the gap.

The New Deal: The First Wave of Dependency

The Great Depression devastated state budgets. With no ability to print money and limited ability to borrow, states turned to Washington for relief.

The New Deal created:

- Social Security
- Unemployment insurance
- Agricultural subsidies
- Public works programs
- Federal infrastructure spending

These programs were funded federally but administered locally, a structure that created the first major **federal-state dependency loop.**

States needed the money.

The federal government needed compliance.

The Great Society: The Expansion of Conditional Funding

The 1960s brought the second wave of dependency.

The Great Society created:

- Medicaid
- Medicare
- Federal education funding
- Housing programs
- Urban development grants

These programs dramatically increased federal spending and with it, federal leverage.

For the first time, federal funds came with conditions:

- adopt federal standards
- follow federal guidelines
- implement federal rules
- report data to federal agencies

States could refuse the money. But refusing meant political suicide. Dependency hardened into structure.

The Highway Act and the Birth of Regulatory Blackmail

The Federal Aid Highway Act of 1956 created the interstate system and with it, a new form of leverage.

Federal highway funds became a tool for:

- shaping state transportation policy
- mandating seatbelt laws
- enforcing national speed limits
- imposing drinking age requirements

The Supreme Court upheld this model in *South Dakota v. Dole* (1987), ruling that Congress could withhold funds to coerce state compliance as long as the conditions were "related" to the program. This ruling legitimized conditional funding as a constitutional tool.
The Beast gained a whip.

Medicaid: The Largest Lever of All

Medicaid became the single largest source of federal leverage over the states.

Because Medicaid is:

- jointly funded
- federally regulated
- state-administered
- politically sensitive
- financially enormous

…it became the perfect mechanism for federal influence.

States depend on Medicaid for:

- hospitals
- nursing homes
- disability services
- mental health care
- low-income coverage

The federal government uses Medicaid to:

- impose coverage mandates
- enforce reporting requirements
- shape state health policy
- expand administrative oversight.

Education Funding: The Federalization of Local Schools

Education was once the most local of all government functions. But federal funding changed that.

Key milestones include:

- Elementary and Secondary Education Act (1965)
- Individuals with Disabilities Education Act (1975)
- No Child Left Behind (2001)
- Race to the Top (2009)

Each program increased federal funding and federal control.

States and school districts became dependent on:

- Title I funds
- special education grants
- testing mandates
- federal accountability systems

The Beast gained access to the classroom.

Disaster Relief and Emergency Powers

Federal disaster relief through FEMA and other agencies became another tool of dependency.

States rely on federal funds for:

- hurricanes
- floods
- wildfires
- pandemics
- earthquakes

But federal relief requires:

- compliance with federal emergency standards
- adherence to federal planning requirements
- cooperation with federal agencies
- acceptance of federal oversight

The Beast gained control over crisis management.

The Grant System: A Web of Financial Control

Today, the federal government distributes over 1,300 grant programs across dozens of agencies.

These grants fund:

- transportation
- housing
- policing
- education
- healthcare
- agriculture
- energy
- environmental protection

Each grant comes with:

- reporting requirements
- compliance mandates
- regulatory obligations
- administrative oversight

States administer the programs.
Federal agencies control the rules.
The Beast gained tentacles.

The States Lose Their Sovereignty

Over time, federal funding became:

- too large to refuse
- too complex to manage independently
- too politically essential to cut
- too intertwined with state budgets to unwind

This created a structural reality: States are no longer sovereign fiscal entities. They are administrative subdivisions of the federal government. The administrative state governs through money. The states comply because they must.
The Beast does not need to command.
It only needs to fund or defund.

The Result: A Nation of Dependents

By the first quarter of the 21st century, the states have become:

- financially dependent
- administratively compliant
- structurally subordinate
- fiscally constrained

- politically vulnerable

The federal government controls:

- the currency
- the credit markets
- the grants
- the conditions
- the oversight
- the enforcement

The states control:

- the paperwork
- the implementation
- the compliance

The Beast gained a bloodstream and the states became its capillaries.

The administrative state did not conquer the states. It purchased them. Through currency control, conditional funding, grant programs, and fiscal leverage, the federal government transformed the states from sovereign entities into dependent administrators.

Congress created the Beast, gave it food.
The courts armored it.
The bureaucracy gave it a mind.
The information monopoly gave it a voice.
The inter-agency shield gave it immunity.
The media gave it legitimacy.
And federal money gave it dominion.

CHAPTER 9
The Illusion of Choice: How Elections Became Performative While the Beast Remained Permanent

Elections are the heartbeat of a republic. They are the ritual through which the people choose their leaders, set the direction of government, and hold power accountable. At least, that is the theory.

In practice, modern American elections have become performative, emotionally charged, media-driven, and symbolically significant, while structurally disconnected from the machinery of governance. Presidents change. Congress changes. Judges change. Governors, mayors, commissioners, city council members all change. But the administrative state, the Beast remains.

The Founders' Model: Elections as the Engine of Accountability

The Founders believed elections would:

- restrain ambition
- correct abuses
- refresh leadership
- reflect public will

- prevent permanent power centers

They assumed that elected officials would:

- write the laws
- control the purse
- oversee the Executive
- direct national policy

They did not imagine a world where:

- Congress delegates its authority.
- Courts defer to agency interpretations.
- Agencies write most binding rules.
- States depend on federal funding.
- Media amplifies official narratives.

In the Founders' model, elections controlled government. In the modern model, elections control *politicians*, not the government.

The Rise of the Permanent Government

The administrative state is permanent. Elections are temporary.

Presidents serve four-year terms.

Senators serve six-year terms.

Representatives serve two-year terms.

Governors serve four-year terms.

But the administrative state serves **forever**.

Career officials remain for:

- Twenty years
- Thirty years
- Forty years
- Fifty plus years

They outlast:

- presidents
- cabinets
- congressional majorities
- judicial appointments
- political movements

This permanence creates a structural imbalance:
Elections change the actors. The administrative state
keeps the script.

The Limits of Presidential Power

Presidents campaign on sweeping promises:

- reform agencies
- cut regulations
- change policy
- reduce bureaucracy
- redirect national priorities

But once in office, they confront the reality:

- Agencies resist rapid change.
- Civil service protections limit removals.
- Internal processes slow everything.
- Inter-agency coordination dilutes directives.
- Courts defer to agency expertise.
- Congress controls funding.
- States control implementation.

A president can:

- appoint agency heads
- issue Executive orders
- set broad priorities

But the administrative state can:

- reinterpret
- delay
- dilute
- resist
- outlast

The Beast does not defy presidents.
It gives them the illusion of power while preventing them from doing any actual damage to the administrative state.

Congress and the Illusion of Legislative Control

Members of Congress campaign on:

- cutting spending
- reforming programs
- limiting agencies
- restoring accountability

But once elected, they face:

- massive omnibus bills
- unreadable continuing resolutions
- agency-written legislative language
- staff shortages
- partisan gridlock
- dependence on agency expertise

Congress rarely writes detailed laws anymore.
It writes frameworks that agencies fill in.
This means: Elections change the legislators. They do not change the legislation.

The States and the Illusion of Federalism

Governors and state legislators campaign on:

- resisting federal overreach
- protecting state sovereignty
- controlling local policy

But states depend on:

- Medicaid funding

- education grants
- transportation money
- disaster relief
- housing subsidies
- law enforcement grants

Refusing federal money is politically impossible.
Accepting it means accepting federal conditions.
This means: Elections change state leaders. They do not change state dependency.

The Media and the Illusion of Narrative Control

Candidates campaign through:

- televised debates
- social media
- cable news
- national outlets

But the media ecosystem:

- prioritizes engagement over accuracy
- amplifies official narratives
- relies on agency data

- depends on institutional access
- nationalizes local issues

This means: Elections change the messaging. They do not change the megaphone.

The Courts and the Illusion of Constitutional Correction

Voters often believe that:

- Courts will restrain agencies.
- Judges will enforce limits.
- Constitutional boundaries will be restored.

But courts:

- avoid political questions
- defer to agency expertise
- rely on administrative records
- move slowly
- rarely overturn major programs

Even major rulings take years to implement and agencies adapt around them, meaning, elections change judicial appointments. They do not change judicial deference.

The Bureaucratic Veto

The administrative state has a subtle but powerful tool: the bureaucratic veto.

It includes:

- selective enforcement
- procedural delay
- slow walking
- reinterpretation
- internal review cycles
- risk-averse legal opinions
- strategic leaks

These tools allow agencies to:

- neutralize directives
- dilute reforms
- stall implementation
- preserve their authority

This veto is not written in law. It is written in culture. And it is immune to elections.

The Public Senses the Disconnect

Over time, voters have noticed:

- Policies don't change much.
- Agencies continue their agendas.
- Regulations expand regardless of elections.
- Federal spending grows under all parties.
- Crises produce the same institutional responses.
- The administrative state remains untouched.

This creates a sense of:

- frustration
- cynicism
- disillusionment
- political fatigue
- declining trust

People feel like elections matter less. They are not imagining it.

The Result: Elections as Ritual, Not Governance

By the first quarter of the 21st century, American elections have become:

- symbolic
- emotional
- media-driven
- high-stakes in appearance
- low-impact in practice

Elections determine:

- who speaks for the government

They do not determine:

- how the government operates
- which policies endure
- which agencies expand
- how money flows
- how rules are written
- how power is exercised

Elections are temporary. The administrative state is permanent.
The Beast does not fear elections.
It is above them.

The illusion of choice is not a conspiracy. It is a structural reality. Elections change the faces. The administrative state keeps the power.

Congress created the Beast, gave it food.
The courts armored it.
The bureaucracy gave it a mind.
The information monopoly gave it a voice.
The inter-agency shield gave it immunity.
The media gave it legitimacy.
Federal money gave it dominion.
And elections gave it cover.

CHAPTER 10
The Beast Ascendant: A System That Serves Itself

By now, the shape of the Beast is unmistakable.

It has a body built by congressional delegation.

It has armor forged by judicial deference.

It has a mind formed by the permanent bureaucracy.

It has a voice through the information monopoly.

It has immunity through inter-agency protection.

It has legitimacy through the media.

It has dominion through federal money.

It has cover through elections.

This chapter explains what all of that adds up to:

a government that no longer responds to the people, but to itself.

Not because of malice.

Not because of conspiracy.

But because of structure.

The administrative state has become a self-directed organism, a system that grows, adapts, and protects itself regardless of who occupies elected office.

This is the Beast ascendant.

The Administrative State as a Living Organism

Every chapter so far has described a different organ, limb, or instinct. But the administrative state is not a collection of parts. It is a **system** interconnected, interdependent, and self-reinforcing.

It behaves like a living organism because:

- It has memory.
- It has continuity.
- It has internal communication.
- It has defensive reflexes.
- It has metabolic needs (funding).
- It has a worldview.
- It has survival instincts.

No single agency controls or restrains it.
No single election redirects it.
The Beast is not commanded.
It simply **is**.

The Shift From Democratic Legitimacy to Institutional Legitimacy

In a constitutional republic, legitimacy comes from:

- elections
- representation
- accountability
- consent of the governed

But the administrative state derives legitimacy from:

- expertise
- continuity
- complexity
- institutional norms
- procedural compliance

This shift is subtle but profound.
Democratic legitimacy asks: **"Did the people choose this?"**
Institutional legitimacy asks: **"Did the process follow the rules?"**
The Beast thrives on the second question.
The first has become irrelevant.

The Triumph of Process Over Outcomes

The administrative state does not measure success by:

- public satisfaction
- democratic approval
- electoral mandates
- constitutional boundaries

It measures success by:

- compliance
- documentation
- procedural correctness
- internal metrics
- regulatory expansion
- budget stability

This is why agencies can:

- fail publicly
- waste billions
- mismanage programs
- produce contradictory rules
- generate public frustration

...and still grow.

The Beast does not need to succeed.

It only needs to continue.

The Absorption of Political Energy

Elections generate enormous political energy through:

- campaigns
- debates
- promises
- movements
- mandates

But once the election ends, that energy is absorbed by the administrative state.

Presidents discover that:

- Agencies reinterpret their directives.
- Courts defer to agency expertise.
- Congress lacks capacity.
- States depend on federal money.
- Media narratives shape public perception.

Political energy dissipates. Institutional inertia prevails. The Beast ignores elections, they are not relevant to it.

The Expansion of Authority Through Crisis

Crises are accelerants.

During:

- wars
- recessions
- pandemics
- natural disasters
- security threats

...the administrative state gains:

- emergency powers
- expanded budgets
- new programs
- broader mandates
- public deference

After the crisis ends, the powers remain.
The Beast grows during storms and never shrinks afterward.

The Disappearance of Accountability

Accountability requires:

- clear lines of authority
- identifiable decision-makers
- transparent processes
- consequences for failure

The administrative state has none of these.

Instead, it has:

- shared responsibility
- overlapping jurisdictions
- opaque processes
- procedural shields
- legal insulation
- political ambiguity

When something goes wrong:

- Agencies blame Congress.
- Congress blames agencies.
- States blame Washington.
- Washington blames states.
- Media blames partisanship.
- Courts blame ambiguity.

Everyone is responsible. Therefore no one is responsible. The Beast cannot be blamed, it only works there.

The Public's Growing Alienation

As the administrative state expands, the public senses that:

- Agencies act independently.
- Elections matter less.
- Policies don't change.
- Crises produce the same responses.
- Spending grows regardless of party.
- Regulations multiply without debate.
- Transparency declines.

This alienation is not apathy. It is recognition, trust has been eroded. People feel disconnected from their government because their government is disconnected from them.
The Beast does not listen.
It broadcasts on all frequencies, twenty-four seven, three sixty-five.

The System That Serves Itself

The administrative state does not serve:

- The President
- Congress
- the courts
- the states
- the voters

It serves:

- its own continuity
- its own authority
- its own worldview
- its own internal incentives

This is not corruption. It is evolution.
The Beast is not evil.
It is indifferent.
It does not hate the public.
It simply does not need to invest any energy in their direction.

The Point of No Return

Every institution reaches a moment when reform becomes impossible because:

- There are no incentives to oppose it.
- The actors are too invested.
- The structures are too entrenched.
- The dependencies are too deep.
- The alternatives are too costly.

The administrative state has reached that moment. Congress cannot reclaim its power. Courts cannot dismantle deference. Presidents cannot control the bureaucracy. States cannot reject federal money. Media will not regain independence. Elections cannot redirect the system.
The Beast is now self-sustaining.

What Comes Next

Is the administrative state malicious? Hard to say with how the word has been legislatively watered down. The primary observations of the book are based on what has historically occurred and what lessons from history do we utilize to fix what is broken.

The question is no longer: "How do we restrain it?"
The question is: "How do we live with it?"

Because the administrative state is now:

- the primary maker of policy
- the interpreter of law
- the enforcer of rules
- the allocator of money
- the manager of crises
- the arbiter of information
- the guardian of its own existence

The Beast is ascendant.
And the republic must now decide whether it will confront that reality or continue pretending that elections alone can tame a creature that no longer answers to them.

EPILOGUE
A System That Outgrew Its Designers

From a distance, the story of the American administrative state does not look like a conspiracy, a coup, or a moral failure. It looks like something far more familiar in the natural world: an organism adapting to survive.

Every institution described in this book—Congress, the courts, the bureaucracy, the media, the states—behaved according to its incentives. None set out to build a system beyond democratic reach. None intended to create a structure that would outlive elections, absorb political energy, and govern through continuity rather than consent.

Yet that is what emerged. **<u>A government designed to be dynamic became static</u>**. A system built on tension settled into equilibrium. A republic meant to be steered by the people became steered by its own inertia set in motion by greedy, cowardly apathetic lizard-brained evolved monkeys with delusions of grandeur.

From a non-political vantage point, the administrative state is neither villain nor hero. It is simply the predictable result of humanity. Modern societies require expertise, continuity, and coordination. They require institutions that do not reset every four years. They require systems that can absorb shocks, manage crises, and maintain stability.

But stability has a cost. The more a system stabilizes itself, the less responsive it becomes. The more it protects itself, the less accountable it becomes. The more it grows, the less it resembles what its designers intended. The administrative state did not seize power. It accumulated it slowly, quietly, structurally. And once accumulated, that power was not returned to its rightful owners.

From a neutral perspective, the story of the Beast is not a story of malice. It is a story of emergence, the way small decisions, made over decades, can produce a structure no one fully controls and few fully understand.
What does a society do when its government becomes something its founders did not anticipate and cannot easily change?
There is no single answer.
There may be many.
Or there may be none.

But the first step is recognition, seeing the system clearly, without illusion, without nostalgia, without fear. Seeing it as it is, not as we wish it to be.

Only then can the people decide what comes next.

Don't forget to check out the
author's website for access to
the rest of his multimedia art

WWW.ALCHEMYANDARTISTRY.COM

ISBN 979-8-9947580-0-7

www.ingramcontent.com/pod-product-compliance
Lightning Source LLC
Chambersburg PA
CBHW070629130626
46555CB00006B/2488